TRIPPING
AMERICA
THE FANTASTIC

Part One
I

By Mark Jager

ZOSMA PUBLICATIONS
P.O. Box 284
Marion, Michigan 49665

TRIPPING AMERICA
THE FANTASTIC
by Mark Jager

Published by
ZOSMA PUBLICATIONS
P.O. Box 284
Maion, Michigan 49601

Design and layout by Deana Jager

Editing by Brenda Hamacher

We would like to thank the following people for their contribution in putting this book together:

Sandy Roundhouse	Melissa Sherwood
Deena Murawski	Kari Westman
Emily Hughes	Jenny Wing

Photo Credits:
Wind Cave National Park
Cahokia Mounds State Historic Site
Charlie Riedel
Iowa National Park Service
Dinosaur State Park
Arkansas Dept. of parks & tourism

Copyright©2002 by Mark A. Jager
First Edition volume 1 2002
ISBN: 0-9672464-7-4
Printed in the U.S.A.

10 9 8 7 6 5 4 3 2 1

DEDICATED TO

This book is dedicated to my wife, Deana,
and my three wonderful children;
Emili, Madelein and Mark Daniel,
for all their love and support.
Whom are the inspiration for all that I do.
I love you.

TABLE OF CONTENTS

ALABAMA
MOUNDVILLE

There is an ancient city in Alabama. Its builders arranged it symmetrically. The city had a central plaza, a central axis, and was laid out with careful planning.

The ancient city was located on the Black Warrior River in Central Alabama. The city covered approximately 300 acres and is estimated to have had a population of nearly 1,000 people. It is the second largest ancient city that has been found in America as far as researchers know.

There are 26 mounds that can be found at the site. One of the structures is a 58-foot tall pyramid. On top of the pyramid is a building which visitors can go into to see a life-size Indian diorama.

There is a museum at the site, complete with exhibits on Indian culture and artifacts. There is also a museum theater. There is a festival at the site that lasts for the first full week of October, the Native American

Festival. There is also a campground at the site. Moundville is located on Highway 69, 15 miles south of Tuscaloosa, Alabama. For more information, call 205-371-2234.

ALASKA
THE VALLEY OF 10,000 SMOKES

In 1912, the Alaskan volcano named Novarupta erupted. It was an unbelievable eruption. Nearly 40 miles were turned into a wasteland. A nearby valley was buried in 500 feet of ash, while the ash was still a foot deep 100 miles away.

It is believed by researchers that the volcano spewed 100 times more material than Mount St. Helen did when it blew. The plume from the volcano is reported to have shot up 20 miles into the sky.

A nearby mountain, Mount Katmai, had the top of it blown right off. It was 6 miles away from the volcano. When the mountain was decapitated, a huge crater was made. Now an incredible crater lake is there, surrounded by 300-foot walls.

In 1916, steam poured out from vents all over the valley. That is how it got its name.

The layers of ash and volcanic rock have cooled. The valley no longer steams. However, it is still a moonscape of ash and volcanic rock. It's an interesting place to go if you want to see a strange landscape.

Contact the Alaskan D.N.R. for more information.

THE RAINBOW FOREST

Nestled in Arizona is a fantastic place that sounds like something out of a fairy tale when you first hear of it, the Rainbow Forest.

The Rainbow Forest is also known as the Petrified Forest. The forest covers over 93,500 acres. It's one of the biggest petrified forests in the world. It is known as the Rainbow Forest because it is one of the most colorful petrified forests on the planet.

The Rainbow Forest has chips of onyx, jasper, and agate. Some of the trunks lying in this area are over 100 feet long. Another interesting feature of the forest is Agate Bridge. Agate Bridge was a huge tree at one time. The tree fell over a deep ravine and petrified into agate. The result is a large natural bridge over 100 feet long over a deep ravine, according to <u>arizonaguide.com</u>. The Painted Desert, with its various shades of color, is also interesting to see, as it is near the forest. Here are archaeological sites which contain fossils that are thousands of years old.

The park goes all the way between I-40 and U.S. 180. Westbound travelers on I-40 can exit at milepost 311, drive through the park and take U.S. 180 at the south end west to Holbrook and continue west on I-40.

Eastbound travelers can exit I-40 at Holbrook and take U.S. 180 east to the park, go north through the park, and return to I-40. For more information call 928-524-6228.

ARKANSAS
THE CRATER OF DIAMONDS

Somewhere in the remote past, a fiery volcano erupted in southwest Arkansas. Emerging out of the blazing and deep vault of the earth came thousands of brilliant, shining diamonds. Now anyone who wants to can go to what is called a volcanic pipe and look for ancient treasures. This is done on a 35-acre site located near Murfreesboro, Arkansas, about a three-hour drive south of Alma. The cost is only $4.50 a day.

While digging through the greenish lamproite soil, you may find diamonds of various colors: white, yellow and brown. The stones are rounded, about the size of a match head-a crystal with a metallic shine to it.

At the Crater of Diamonds, you have a chance to discover a variety of dazzling stones. Some of these stones are: jasper, which is round, dull and waxy appearing; amethyst, which is purple quartz; agate, which when cut reveals beautiful patterns; calcite, a milky white mineral with crystal shapes; and barite, which comes in a variety of different colors.

The Crater of Diamonds is located 2 ½ miles from Murfreesboro on Highway 301. For more information, call 870-285-3113

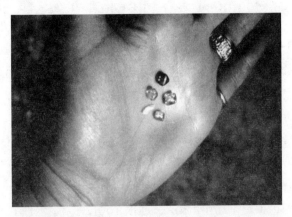

CALIFORNIA
MYSTERY WALL

In the hills east of San Francisco are lengthy walls made from tightly constructed basalt boulders, some of which exceed a ton. The walls extend for miles along the crests of hills from Milpitas to Berkeley. The walls are thought by some to run between 20 and 50 miles, as the remains of them can still be seen in various places.

These walls are hundreds, perhaps thousands, of years old. Nobody seems to know who built them or why they were built. Are these walls the remnants of an ancient civilization from the Annedeluvian World?

There have been a variety of theories as to who built them. Some say they were built by the people of Atlantis, others say the Indians, or even ancient astronauts built them.

Some of the boulders from the walls can still be seen at various locations. One of the places they can be seen is at Tilden Regional Park. Researchers observe parts of the walls on Vollmer Peak. It is even easier to find two large wall boulders in Tilden's Botanical Garden.

At one time the two stones were part of a wall south of the garden. The wall was destroyed during construction in the 1930's. In 1969, an ancient buried water tunnel is reported to have been found there.

COLORADO
CAVE OF THE WINDS

At Cave of the Winds in Colorado, you can experience the best of both the natural and the technological world.

There are three different tours available at the cave. One of the tours takes visitors through 20 spectacular cave rooms. The caverns are lit up with colorful lights. This adds a dazzling flare to an already beautiful natural environment.

There is also a tour you can take which is by lantern light. This is called the historic tour. There is a further tour called the Explorer's Trip. On the Explorer's Trip, you explore a rugged cave and have to wear a helmet.

Laser Canyon is the technological aspect of the experience. At the canyon, you sit 500 feet above the canyon floor. A mesmerizing laser show flashes across the canyon creating a fantastic atmosphere of colorful lights and shadow.

There are various rooms to be seen in the cave: Canopy Hall, the largest room, is 200 feet long and 60 feet wide. The Bridal Chamber, has beautiful stalagmites and stalactites. The Temple of Silence is a room of various formations. The Valley of Dreams contains a colorful flowstone formation called The Painted Curtain. There is also a beautiful location called Oriental Gardens.

Cave of the Winds is open every day. The Laser Canyon show can be seen from Memorial Day to Labor Day weekend. The cave is located 6 miles west of Colorado Springs on Highway 24, exit 141. For more information call 719-685-5444.

CONNECTICUT
DINOSAUR
TRACK WAY

Do you want to take your children to see dinosaur footprints? Go to a museum, right? Well, maybe, but if you really want to see dinosaur footprints as they existed naturally, go to the Connecticut Valley.

The Connecticut Valley is well known for its high number of preserved dinosaur footprints. Millions of years ago dinosaurs walked through the shallow mud flats, leaving their footprints. The area now has been turned into gray sandstone. Some of the top layers of sandstone have been removed, for various reasons, exposing the ancient rock.

There are also ancient plant remains and other things that can be found at the site. If you would like to visit this location, you'll have to first travel to Rocky Hill, Connecticut. Dinosaur State Park is about 1 mile east off I-91, Exit 23.

The telephone number is 860-529-8423.

19

DELAWARE
COIN BEACH

Talk about gifts from the sea! There is a beach in Delaware where money washes ashore after each severe storm. This is strange, but true.

A beach just north of the Indian River Inlet is known to some as Coin Beach. This is because thousands of coins have washed ashore there. The coins were issued under the reign of King George III of England. The dates of the coins range from 1774 to 1782. They come from an 1800's shipwreck.

During the 1930's, the United States Coast Guard found thousands of coins. Today many organized groups make planned visits to the site to search for coins. Most of the coins found were copper; however, some of the coins were silver and gold. Most of the silver coins were Spanish pillar dollars and neales and the gold coins were English rose guineas.

Coin Beach is located near the Indian River Inlet, just south of Lewes, Delaware.

THE CORAL CASTLE

There is a strange place you can visit in Homestead, Florida. It is called Coral Castle.

A Latvian recluse named Edward Leedskalnin constructed an entire complex of monolithic blocks of coral called the Coral Castle.

The strange thing about it is, he did it all by himself. Some of the blocks weighed 30 tons. Somehow, he put them in place single-handedly. The average stone block in his structure weighed more than the average block in the Great Pyramid. It took Edward 28 years to complete the monument. When he was finished he had placed 1,100 tons of rock in place.

Edward also did most of his work in the dark by torchlight. None of his neighbors seemed to see what he was doing. The castle walls weighed about 15 tons each. He had a monstrous 30-ton rock crowned with a gable. He also built a 3-ton rocking chair, a 9-ton gate, a 23-ton Jupiter block, a 22-ton moon block, a 22-ton obelisk and other features.

People from various fields came to him hoping to find out how he had accomplished building the castle by himself. He never told anybody and he took his secret with him to the grave.

Now you and your family can visit the Coral Castle for yourself. When in Florida, take Interstate 95 south to its end then follow U.S. 1 to Coral Castle. For more information call 305-248-6344.

GEORGIA
FORT MOUNTAIN

On top of a mountain in northern Georgia is a strange and uncanny ancient wall.

The wall is reported by researchers to be 885 feet long. It is said to be 7 feet tall at its tallest point, and at one place is up to 12 feet wide. Many believe that the structure predates the Indians.

Many scholars reportedly believe that the wall may be 900 years old. There is an absence of religious artifacts at the site. Some believe it was part of an ancient astronomical device, and that the wall runs east and west around a precipice. The state of Georgia has recognized the structure and placed a monument in a nearby location.

Some believe it was built by the Welsh explorer Prince Madoc Ab Owain Gwynedd.

The ancient wall is located in Fort Mountain State Park near the Cohutta Wilderness Area in northern Georgia. It is an interesting place to take pre-Columbian history buffs.

Take I-75 north, Exit 293, Highway 41 north to Chatsworth. The park is located 8 miles east of Chatsworth on Highway 52.

HAWAII
LAVA TREE PARK

Thousands of years ago, a volcano erupted in Hawaii. Ash and debris floated down over tropical forests like snowflakes and covered the trees, creating what looked like a volcanic winter.

The volcanic ash hardened on the trees. Over thousands of years the Master Artist sent rains and wind to erode away the unhardened debris. The trees, now called Lava Trees were left. These volcanic trees made a lasting record of an ancient tropical forest.

The park is a favorite for locals. It is located not far from Pahoa on the road that divides to take you to Kapoho or Pohoiki.

IDAHO
CRATERS
OF THE MOON

Craters of the Moon is a place in Idaho that looks like the surface of the moon. Some have described it as being some of the strangest terrain in North America.

Craters of the Moon covers 83 square miles. It was formed by ancient volcanoes. There are odd surface patterns and formations formed from basaltic lava flows. There isn't just one volcano, there are many. Many fissure vents, volcanic cones, and lava flows spewed forth lava, and a weird lunar landscape was formed in the area. A number of astronomy parties take place in the strange region. The astronauts trained for the moon landing there.

You can drive a 7-mile loop road to discover various spatter and cinder cones, lava flows, and lava tube caves. There are several different areas in the craters area that have actually been named. North Crater Flow is an area of monoliths or crater wall fragments that can be observed. Further down the road is North Crater Trail. This long steep trail leads to a place where you can look into a volcano vent.

Other sites to observe are the Orchard, which are lava fragments which set like islands in the midst of numerous cinders and Inferno Cone Viewpoint, which is a whole landscape of cinder cones which spread out to a distant mountain horizon. There is also Big Cinder which is one of the largest basaltic cinder cones on the planet, as well as the spatter cones area, and the tree molds area. The tree molds area is a location where lava molded around trees. The trees then decayed leaving only the mold of trees standing. The last stop on the loop road will take you to the lava tubes. Here you can explore various caves. These include Beauty, Boy Scout, Dew-drop, Surprise Caves, and the Indian Tunnel.

To get to Craters of the Moon and to drive down the loop road, which will take you to these sites, take Highway 26 from Blackfoot, Idaho, to Arco. At Arco; Highway 26 will intersect with Highway 20. Take Highway 20 west about 20 miles.

ILLINOIS
THE AMERICAN PYRAMID

Did you know that there are pyramids in America that you can visit at any time?

In Illinois are the remnants of an ancient city, which researchers today call Cahokia. The western Illinois site is the largest known prehistoric site in America. It is believed that the city covered 6 square miles, and its population ranged between 8,000 to 40,000 people.

The city was laid out in rows. The central plaza of the city featured stepped pyramid temples. At the center was a huge pyramid now called Monks Mound. Monks Mound is the largest prehistoric construction in America. It is 100 feet tall. The four tiered platform is believed to have been built over a period of 300 years. Its base covers more than 14 acres.

It is believed by some researchers that

the town flourished between 1050-1150 A.D.
Its builders mysteriously vanished. The
pyramid is open for visitors.

To get to Cahokia, take I-64 to I-255
North. Take I-255 north to Exit 24,
Collinsville Road. Turn left on road at
stoplight at end of off ramp.

INDIANA
UNDERGROUND
WATERFALLS

You can take a journey into the ancient past. You can observe the rippling secret waterways of the earth; a secret treasure of God hidden in the depths of the earth, in the fountains of the deep.

Sculptured cave formations surround underground streams which smoothly flow over rare and spectacular underground waterfalls. Still further into this subterranean world are what one may call spectacular dazzling rock gardens. Stalactites, stalagmites, flowstone and other rocks fascinate you in this grand cathedral. These icicles of rock make spectacular viewing for a colorful, pleasant family trip.

For more information, call 812-732-4382. Near Corydon, Indiana, take 135 South 12 ½ miles. You will see a large yellow billboard on the left side, Corydon Entrance Road. Turn left and go to Squire Boon Road, 3 ½ miles to park.

IOWA
EFFIGY MOUNDS

As you are traveling in Iowa you may want to visit the Effigy Mounds; strange, unusual animal patterns built into the ground by Native Americans.

When approaching the formations, you will see off in the distance low rises on the landscape. These ripples in the distance soon formulate in your vision into regular patterns in the hills. Tracing the patterns, the "hills" soon turn into recognizable shapes; they are animals of various kinds.

These ceremonial mounds represent a number of animals. These include eagles, falcons, bison, deer, turtles, lizards, and bears. In 1949, the Effigy Mounds became a recognized national monument. The monument preserves a very important aspect of Native American history.

The Effigy Mounds are located at 151 Highway 76, Harpers Ferry, Iowa. For more information call 563-873-3491.

33

KANSAS
THE CHALK PYRAMIDS

Out on the prairies of Kansas in southwest Gove County are strange rock towers called the Chalk Pyramids.

The Chalk Pyramids are also known as Monument Rocks. They once served as landmarks for pioneers. Some of the formations are 60 feet high.

The Chalk Pyramids are a very surprising element to the landscape. For miles around all there is is a vast prairie, and then suddenly, out of nowhere, appear vast outcroppings of rock on both sides of the road.

The two sets of towering limestone formations that rise out of the prairie are thought by researchers to be from the times of the dinosaurs. It is believed that thousands of years ago western Kansas was covered by hundreds of feet of water. In time the water receded, and all the erosion left were the pyramids of rock known as Monument Rocks. The site of Monument Rock is remote. The closest town is Healy, which is 15 miles to the southeast. Gove is 17 miles to the northeast. Oakley is 25 miles to the northwest, and Scott City is 23 miles to the southeast.

If you would like to visit the Chalk Pyramids in Kansas, go on I-70, take Exit 76 at Oakley and head south 20 miles on U.S. Highway 83 until its junction with Jayhawk Road, north of the Smoky Hill River. Take the road 4 miles east, then follow it to the south for 3 miles. The road turns east again for another mile, then south once more.

36

KENTUCKY

THE MOONBOW

Hidden in Kentucky, nestled in a corner of the great outdoors, is a phenomenon of nature which takes place at Cumberland Falls.

Here a bizarre event takes place which has an astronomical connection. You can't see this show of nature every night. In fact, it only takes place by the light of a bright full moon. What is it? One of the world's few Moonbows.

As the 125-foot wide falls drop 60 feet into a gorge on the boulders below, it throws up a huge spray. In the glow of the light of the full moon, a moonbow is often produced.

A moonbow is different than a rainbow. The beams of light arising from the mist appear different to every person who sees it. This depends on the angle of perception from which a person is observing it. Some people see it as a beam of white light. Others see hazes of red and blue at the sides. Regardless of how people see it, it is very mesmerizing.

To get to Cumberland Falls, take South Interstate 75 out of Lexington close to Williamsburg, Kentucky. Follow the signs.

LOUISIANA
MARKSVILLE MOUNDS

There are remnants of an ancient settlement near Marksville, Louisiana. Some researchers believe it is nearly 1,400 years old.

The historic site covers 42 acres. There are strange earthen structures built by the ancient inhabitants of the settlement at the site. The main portion of the settlement is surrounded by a huge ancient earthen wall. The rounded wall is 3,300 feet long and is between 3 to 7 feet tall. There are openings in this "wall," two on the southern side, and one on the western side, according to researchers.

Within the huge earthen wall are a variety of earthen shapes. The most northerly mound is 300 feet in diameter and about 13 feet high.

Two conical shaped earthworks sit near the center of the huge semicircular wall. One of them is 100 feet across and 20 feet high.

Another mound is 70 feet across but only 3 ½ feet high.

In the southern section of the semicircular wall is a structure that is thought to have been a huge rectangular formation nearly 285 feet by 235 feet and around 14 feet tall. There are other mounds that have been somewhat destroyed by farming.

Now you can visit this strange site for yourself. It is located east of LA 1 adjacent to the town of Marksville, southeast of Alexandria. From LA 1, turn onto Preston Street (LA 452) and head northeast, then right onto Martin Luther King Drive. Continue until you see the park. The telephone numbers are 318-253-8954 or 888-253-8954.

MAINE

THUNDER HOLE

Mt. Desert Island, located in the Penobscot Bay of Maine, contains an unusual phenomenon called Thunder Hole.

Thunder Hole is a cleft in the ocean cliffs located on the eastern side of Mt. Desert Island. Ocean waves travel down the channel in the cleft. Large beach-ball-sized rocks tumble in the channel. Air is forced by the waves to the end of the channel. At this point, large pockets of air are trapped and explode. This produces loud thundering claps, thus the name "Thunder Hole."

To get to Thunder Hole, take Maine Route 3, south 1 mile east of Ellsworth to Bar Harbor. Take Route 233 west for 1.1 miles. The entrance to the park is on your right. You will loop back over a bridge to proceed southward. After .4 miles, turn left on Park Loop Road. Go about 10 miles to a toll station. Follow the signs.

WYE OAK PARK

How would you like to visit the biggest oak tree in the United States? Wye Oak State Park in Maryland is a 27-acre park that features the largest oak tree in America.

Although reports on the size of the tree vary according to several different sources, information is available from the D.N.R. of Maryland.

Department of Natural Resources information states that the tree is a white oak. This tree is measured at 79 feet high and has a crown of 102 feet across. The tree is reported to be 31 feet in circumference 4 feet up on its trunk. The tree is believed to be 460 years old. This area is stated to be an excellent place to have a picnic with your family.

Wye Oak Park can be found on the eastern shore in Talbot County on Maryland Route 662, about 1 mile from the intersection of Route 50 and Route 404.

MASSACHUSETTS
CIRCULAR STONE CHAMBER

As pioneers near Upton, Massachusetts, were clearing land or making their way through the forests of Massachusetts, they stumbled across something astonishing.

There, before their eyes, was some kind of strange and ancient stone formation. With eyes wide open, perhaps hearts pounding, they entered it. It was some kind of a building.

They made their way down a stone passageway. They had gone a full 15 feet when they went through a doorway. To their amazement, it was some kind of a circular chamber. What was it? Some kind of a room, a chamber which was about 11 by 10feet with a strange domed roof.

Perhaps an eerie feeling came over them as they ran back to the settlement to tell others. As early as the 1800's, people were speculating that the fortress was built by a society that predated the Indians. To this day, most are baffled as to what the structure actually is or who built it. The formation is located near Upton, Massachusetts. Go west on Route 135 about 3.5 miles until the road forks; go left. Soon it will intersect with River Street. Turn left on River Street, then right on Elm Street. If you get lost for some reason, ask a local where it is. Then get permission from landowner before observing. We suggest contacting a local historian for more information.

MICHIGAN
SANILAC PETROGLYPHS

Ancient writings carved into the earth, called petroglyphs, may be observed in Michigan. They were discovered in the 1880s when a forest fire burned away brush and grass along the banks of the Cass River in the thumb area of eastern Michigan.

After the forest fire, more than one hundred figures of birds, animal, tracks, spirals, crosses and waves were exposed. The most notable figure is a deeply carved figure of a warrior with his feet apart and his bow drawn.

The purpose of the carvings is unknown. It is speculated that the patterns may have been made by medicine men or by an ancient artist. There is now a 240-acre park at the site. A pavilion protects the most expressive of the designs. Those seeking more information should contact the D.N.R. Parks

Division in Lansing, Michigan.

To get to the Sanilac Petroglyphs, you must know that it is located south of Bad Axe, Michigan. Take M-53 to the Bay City-Forestville Road; then proceed east to Germainia Road and turn south. The parking lot is located on the west side of Germainia Road, about one-half mile south of the Bay City-Forestville Road intersection. Call 517 373-1979 for more information.

MINNESOTA
JEFFER'S PETROGLYPHS

If you're in Minnesota, you may want to stop in and see Jeffer's Petroglyphs.

According to the Minnesota Historical Society, the petroglyphs tell a story that spans over 5,000 years. There are a number of reasons why the Native Americans made the rock art; among them are showing the importance of hunting in their lives, relating their ceremonies, and keeping track of historic events.

The rocks that the petroglyphs are written on are on the open prairie. Some of the different designs depict deer, buffalo, thunderbirds, arrows, turtles, and others. The carvings were made with hammer stones. The Historical Society states that they appear to range in dates from 3,000 B.C to 1750, A.D.

If you would like to visit Jeffers Petroglyphs, they are located near Comfrey and Windom, Minnesota. They are 3 miles east of U.S. Highway 71 on Cottonwood County Road 10, then one mile south on County Road 2. The telephone number is 507-628-5591.

MISSISSIPPI
ANCIENT
PETRIFIED FOREST

In the library of nature is the record of an ancient primeval forest that has been preserved for our space-age generation.

Giant trees, which once stood side by side in a vast woodland cathedral, have undergone a transformation. They have metamorphosed into age-old timbers of stone.

The forest is located in Flora, Mississippi. There is a trail in the forest that is nearly 6 blocks long. There are different interesting petrified logs to see along the way.

At the location there is also a museum, rock shop, gemstone fluming, colorful badlands, and many other interesting things to see.

This forest is the only petrified forest in the eastern United States. It serves as a great educational opportunity for you and your family, friends, or loved ones. It is located in Flora, Mississippi. To get there, go on Highway 49 north of Jackson, Mississippi. For more information call 601-879-8189.

ELEPHANT ROCKS

Have you ever wondered what it would be like to see a train of petrified elephants? Well, maybe petrified elephants are out of the question. The next closest thing is Elephant Rocks State Park in Missouri.

At Elephant Rocks State Park there are giant granite rocks that are grouped in a row. The rounded smoothness of the rocks causes them to slightly resemble a herd of petrified elephants; that is, if you use your imagination.

One of the largest rocks is named Dumbo. The D.N.R. of Missouri reports that the rock weighs approximately 680 tons. There is a picnic area at the site. It's a good location to stop and relax at with your fellow travelers.

For more information call the Missouri Department of Natural Resources at 800-334-6946.

To get to Elephant Rocks, go from Ironton, Missouri, 7 miles north on Highway 21, then 1 mile west on NA, following signs for the park.

MONTANA
GRASSHOPPER
GLACIER

Montana is the home of an oddity known as Grasshopper Glacier.

On the bear-toothed mountain range is a glacier. The glacier is nearly 1 mile long and ½ mile wide. This would not be incredible in and of itself. However, this glacier is not normal. Embedded within the ice of the glacier are millions and millions of grasshoppers which can be seen by the naked eye.

It is believed that they became embedded in the ice when huge swarms of them became frozen while passing over the mountain range and were deposited on the glacier. Building ice and snow buried them. Later, the ice began to melt and exposed the trapped insects. Scientists estimate that the type of grasshoppers caught in the ice were migratory locusts and have been extinct for about 200 years.

To visit Grasshopper Glacier from Cook City, go 1 ½ mile west on Highway 212. Look for a sign that says "to Goose Lake." Turn left on Forest Road 3230 and follow the road, continuing north about 5 miles. The road will end, and then you must hike the remaining 4 miles. For more information or directions call 406-888-7800. Call 307-344-7381 to contact Yellowstone or 406-587-6701 or 406-446-2103 to contact the National Forest.

NEBRASKA
CAR HENGE

Nearly 4,000 years ago, a group of people went to the Salisbury Plain in England and constructed an incredible ancient calendar, now known as stonehenge.

Thousands of years later, a group of people at a family reunion got together and built another one. It replicates Stonehenge in its dimensions and orientation. There is a big difference, however. This monument is in Nebraska and it's made out of old junk cars.

Talk about modern (or is it ancient?) art! The CarHenge is from cars buried in the ground, pointing in an upright position. Then, other cars are placed horizontally across the vertically standing cars to create crossbars.

Jim Renders dreamed up this idea. He once owned the farm on which the CarHenge now stands. The structure was dedicated in 1987 during the summer solstice. The monument is located in Alliance, Nebraska.

To get to CarHenge, go to Alliance, Nebraska. It is located 2 ½ miles North on Highway 87.

NEVADA
VALLEY OF FIRE

About 30 miles northeast of Las Vegas, Nevada, is a strange and mysterious place called the Valley of Fire. The valley is in the desert near an area close to the north end of Lake Mead.

There, the entire landscape is red. In the evening an unusual phenomenon takes place. At sunset, the valley begins to glow a very deep red. From a distance the rocks take on the appearance of being on fire. The whole valley appears to be ablaze. The effect made is striking when viewed in contrast to the Black Hills, which surround it.

The area is filled with petrified dunes, strangely shaped rocks, and sandstone cliffs. In the valley there are various geological oddities including petrified logs, beehives (which are layered sandstone mounds), Mouses Tank, and the white dome.

There are also ancient petroglyphs in the Valley of Fire. Researchers believe that a strange culture called the Anasazi wrote the petroglyphs. The culture is believed to have disappeared from the area around 1250 A.D., leaving no clues as to why they left, or where they went. One of the petroglyphs is thought to depict the event of the crab nebula going super nova in 1054 A.D. The valley is located on state road SSR 167.

NEW HAMPSHIRE
THE AMERICAN STONEHENGE

Nearly 40 miles north of Boston stands a megalithic mystery. On a hillside in New Hampshire are 30 acres containing a number of low walls, cave like primitive buildings, and tunnels.

The builders of the stone monuments are unknown, although theories prevail. Some researchers believe they were used as astronomical observatories, and claim that the structures have astronomical alignments, which include the summer solstice.

Some of the stones at the American Stonehenge weigh tons; the largest stone weighs about 11 tons. Underneath one of the stones is a shaft 8 feet long, which leads to an underground chamber.

There are some who think that the structure was built thousands of years ago by unknown ancient people. Still others theorize that ancient Greek or Phoenician travelers built it. They have noted that there is a similarity between the construction in New Hampshire and that of ancient temples in Malta and Greece.

Directions: To get to the American Stonehenge, take I-93 in New Hampshire to Exit 3. Then take Route 111 east for 4 ½ miles. Follow the signs.

NEW JERSEY
THE PAULINSKILL VIADUCT

There's a huge abandoned bridge out in the woods near Knowlton, New Jersey, in Warren County.

It could be one of the strangest bridges in the country. The bridge was constructed for the railroad. It was made in 1909, and when it was, it was the largest of its kind in the world.

The bridge is nearly 1,100 feet long. It is 115 feet above the Paulinskill River. The bridge is filled with various tunnels. Once a person has climbed into the structure, they can explore its various passageways. It's almost as if people can go caving. The strange thing about the cave is it is manmade and was abandoned nearly 20 years ago.

Another odd thing about it is that the bridge is somewhat hidden. A person visiting the bridge may not notice it and then suddenly it's there. It's not an attraction that many people visit. It is, however, a unique off- the-beaten trail place to visit if you happen to be in the area.

NEW MEXICO
WHITE SANDS MONUMENT

Millions of tiny sparkling grains of white sand ripple and form waves and crests on a magnificent pure white ocean. The winds of time blow over the shifting, pure grains of sand. Tiny granules, grains of sand, move from one area to another like migrating travelers.

This is what you see at the Tularosa Basin, at the northern end of the Chihuahuan Desert, a desert of gypsum dunes, which are as white as snow.

Hypnotic waves of lily-white sand dunes ripple from horizon to horizon. The sands have engulfed 275 square miles. Here lies the world's largest gypsum dune field. Even some of the animals have transformed into a white coloration that camouflages them in the gypsum sand.

The grains of white sand move slowly

across the desert, Continuing a journey that has lasted for countless centuries. A timeless feeling emerges. White Sands Monument is located near Alamogordo, New Mexico.

NEW YORK
BALANCED ROCK

When pioneers first came to New York, they were intrigued by a strange object in the wilderness near North Salem.

There they discovered something that baffles people even today. What they found was a rock formation. The stone structure consisted of a huge boulder evenly and perfectly balanced, setting on top of three small triangular limestones. The boulder weighs over 90 tons. Its measurements are 16 x 14 x 10 feet.

People have no idea how the 90-ton boulder came to rest on the smaller rocks. Some, however, have their theories. There are those who have stated that the stone formation was caused by the great flood in the days of Noah. Mighty torrents of water moved the rock, and when it came to rest, it was on top of three small stones.

Others believe it is a glacial remnant or even an ancient Celtic monument. Whatever it is, it is an interesting sight. The balanced rock is found near North Salem, New York. From North Salem, go east on Hardscrabble Road. Then, veer right onto June Road. Then, go left on Baxter Road (south-east Baxter). Baxter Road will take you to Crane Corner. From there, turn right on Route 116 (Titicus Road). When you come to a fork, stay right on Titicus Road. Go a short distance past Keeler Lane. There you will soon come upon balanced rock.

NORTH CAROLINA
THE BROWN MOUNTAIN LIGHTS

A strange and unusual lighting phenomenon takes place in North Carolina. Bizarre orbs of light appear at random times in the skies over Brown Mountain.

The lights move up and down in the sky without any explanation. They can be seen on a distant horizon over the foothills of the Blue Ridge. The lights look like flying stars that have a blue or red tint.

The lights have been investigated at different times by various groups, such as the U.S. Geological Survey and the Weather Bureau. The United States Forest Service actually has a sign set up at one of the viewing areas. According to a report, the Indians were already witnessing the lights 800 years ago. Everyone has a different theory about what causes the lights.

There are various places in America where you can go to see strange lighting phenomenon.

NORTH DAKOTA
MEDICINE HOLE

On Killdeer Mountain, 10 miles north of Killdeer, North Dakota, is an unusual hole called Medicine Hole.

Medicine Hole is a narrow passageway that leads into a cave that goes down into Killdeer Mountain. Air currents blast upward out of the hole on cold mornings. A fog also rises up out of it.

In the late 1800's, the United States Army was fighting the Sioux Indians. The Army defeated the Indians. Groups of surviving Indians ran into the Killdeer Mountains and were surrounded by the Army. Suddenly, the Indians vanished, without a trace. Later the hole was discovered and it is thought the Indians escaped into the strange hole.

Some years later, the hole was dynamited shut. Eventually it was blasted open again. The result is that a lot of rock fell down into the shafts, and plugged them. The furthest anyone has ever reported to have descended into the hole is 175 feet. Explorers report a strong breeze blowing out from the cracks of the rock. No one knows where the cave would lead if it were opened, or if the Indians escaped through it.

According to some researchers, Medicine Hole can be seen by traveling from Highway 22 north of Killdeer. Take a small gravel road at mile marker 110. The road goes west and ends at a ranch. There is a small campground there. A trail leads to Medicine Hole.

THE GREAT SERPENT MOUND

The Great Serpent Mound, located in Adams County, Ohio, is a remnant of the pre-historic world. No one knows who designed the serpent.

The serpent is a huge mound made out of earth. The terrain is bizarre. The formation is hundreds of feet in length. It dips in its midsection, and then rises at its tail.

In the last century, researchers have started to study the structure. Some have claimed to have uncovered a few of its hidden secrets. A few of them have claimed that the serpent mound is a huge ancient astronomical calendar. Also, there are gravitational and magnetic phenomena that take place there that make it difficult to determine magnetic north.

Some researchers such as Robert Fletcher and Terry Cameron believe that certain stars and planets line up with the head, coils and helix of the serpent at specific times of the year.

Clark and Marjorie Hardman showed that a line of vision facing northwest bisecting the great oval at the head of the effigy marked the line of the setting sun on the summer solstice. William F. Romain discovered that the main events in a 18.6-year lunar cycle can be traced through 6 out of 7 of the serpent coils.

In short, this earthwork has the principles of astronomy, geometry, and numbers incorporated into its design. Some scholars believe that comparisons can be made between America's Serpent Mound and Stonehenge in England. There are also those who believe that the Serpent Mound and Stonehenge were designed by the same people and have been designed together to tell a story. They claim that both of the structures were designed at the same time. The idea is that the Serpent Mound has a unique integration of information on solar and lunar movements inherent in its design. Stonehenge views similar astronomical events. Some state that the two have a harmonious relationship and complement each other. The idea is that the Great Serpent is the guardian or protector of Stonehenge and that Stonehenge is the focal point of the mathematical message being conveyed by the Serpent Mound.

The Serpent Mound is located off of State Route 73, in Peebles, Ohio. Call 937-587-2796 for more information.

OKLAHOMA
ALABASTER
CAVERNS

Enter a brilliant, sparkling world of shining, colorful glass in the heart of the earth. Alabaster Caverns State Park in Oklahoma is the home to an underground land of glass.

Alabaster Caverns is the largest gypsum cave in the world open for public viewing. The cave is ¾ of a mile long. Its incredible rock and mineral formations are rare and cannot be found too many places on the planet.

Massive boulders of alabaster are found in the cave. Alabaster is a fine grained mass gypsum. It comes in a variety of colors, including pink, white, and even a rare black.

There are guided tours of the main cave year round from 8:00 a.m. to 4:00 p.m. Average temperature in the cave is about 50 degrees. There is a perennial stream flowing through the cave. It is supplied by a system of lateral tunnels. This tiny brook, is all that is left of a huge river that once flowed through the cave. You can still see some of the sculptured gypsum formations which it left. The cave is also the home of five species of bats.

Alabaster Caverns is six miles south of Freedom on Highway 50, then ½ mile on Highway 50A, or 27 miles northeast of Woodward on Highway 50. For more information, call 580-621-3381.

OREGON
THE PUNCH BOWL

In Oregon, there is a huge punchbowl made of a hollow rock formation. Researchers believe the punch bowl was formed when a cave roof fell in over a couple of sea caves. The waves from the Pacific Ocean then crashed into the cavern and shaped it.

As the surf violently comes into the punch bowl during winter storms, it is an awesome spectacle. The waters churn, swirl, and create massive amounts of foam. It takes on the appearance of a giant punchbowl.

There are tide pools at the punchbowl area. These are interesting. You can also go to this location to watch whales. The punchbowl is off US 101, 8 miles N. of Newport, Oregon.

PENNSYLVANIA
RINGING ROCKS

In the forests of Pennsylvania is heard the ringing of an ancient song. The song has been heard for thousands of years. Prehistoric tribes heard it; the settlers of William Penn listened to its tones. What is it? It's the sound of ringing rocks.

There is an area in Bucks County, Pennsylvania, where huge rocks ring out like chimes when they are struck with a hammer. The tones vary in range and pitch from a ping to a large bell. The area is called "Ringing Rocks."

The rocks lie scattered across two acres. They have been there since the world was young. The strange thing about them is that they seem to have come from nowhere. They are igneous rocks, and there is no evidence of any volcanic activity in the area. Oddly, two acres of ringing stones are just sitting there in the middle of a typical Pennsylvania forest. There is a similar area located just outside of

Pottstown, Pennsylvania.

To get to the Ringing Rocks locations, these directions will be helpful. At the intersection of Route 32 and Route 611 at Kintersville take Route 32 south to Narrows Hill Road to Ringing Rocks Road. Another area of ringing rocks is located just outside of Pottstown by Route 663.

RHODE ISLAND
THE STONE TOWER

For centuries an age-old stone tower has perched atop a hill, overlooking Newport Harbor in Newport, Rhode Island. Standing like a watchman awaiting the arrival of some ancient mariner, a beacon of a long forgotten time, the tower relays its timeless message.

Where did it come from? Who built it? The only witness of its builders is the ocean, which has long kept its secret.

There have been whispers that the stone formation was built by Norsemen, ancient Phoenicians, or even that it is a long forgotten monument to Yahweh, built by Hebrews long ago. Some say that Benedict Arnold built it. If he did there is no record of it. He took his secret with him to the grave. The structure is built on 8 columns and arches. Some researchers think it is nearly 1,000 years old.

It has been reported that there are other structures buried in the tower's immediate vicinity. Some believe it is connected to a network of other structures. Was this an ancient and forgotten city? Do the depths of earth hide an enigmatic portion of American history? Only time may tell.

You can see this strange tower for yourself. It can be found in Touro Park on Mill Street in Newport, Rhode Island. If you want more information, you can call the Newport Chamber of Commerce at 800-458-4843.

SOUTH CAROLINA
CAESAR'S HEAD

When in South Carolina, Caesar's Head is a good place to visit. There is a large natural rock formation at this location. What is the natural rock formation? It is a large rock that looks like Caesar's head.

At the location there are panoramic views. There is a site called table rock that is interesting. Another interesting feature of the area is Raven Cliff Falls. Raven Cliff Falls is one of the highest waterfalls in the eastern United States.

There are plenty of things to do in this area, including hiking, fishing and camping.

Caesar's Head Park is located on U.S. 276, 37 miles northeast of Greenville near the South Carolina- North Carolina border and five miles from South Carolina Highway 11.

For more information call *864-836-6115*

SOUTH DAKOTA
WIND CAVE

There is a place in America where the earth actually acts like it's breathing, by inhaling and exhaling,air.

This place of the breathing earth was already known long ago. According to reports, the Lakota Indians had a legend which speaks of a hole in the Black Hills that blew air.

Nobody knows exactly how the cave was discovered. Rumors suggest that it was discovered by a pioneer named Tom Bingham in 1881. According to the story, he was out hunting deer when he heard a strange whistling sound in the distance. He found out that it was caused by wind escaping through a small hole in some rocks. The present opening to the cave was made by simply digging down several feet to a number of galleries and corridors filled with different types of crystals.

Strong winds blow in and out of the cave's mouth. This is a very strange phenomenon. Some people believe that it is caused by changes in the pressure of the atmosphere outside. They believe that an outward blowing of wind is caused by a falling barometer and a rising barometer causes the cave to suck the air in. The end result is that the earth appears to be breathing by inhaling one breath for hours and then exhaling that same one breath for hours.

You can observe this phenomenon for yourself.

While traveling on I-90, at Rapid City, South Dakota, exit onto U.S. Route 79 South. Follow Route 79 South about 50 miles to Route 18. Turn right on U.S. Route 385 North. This takes you through Hot Springs and into Wind Cave National Park. Follow the signs.

The park can also be reached by following U.S. Route 16 West out of Rapid City onto U.S. Route 385 South. Call 605-745-4600 for more information.

TENNESSEE
THE LOST SEA

For centuries, a mountain in Tennessee held a secret. Within the depths of the mountain near Sweetwater lies hidden an incredible watery world known as the Lost Sea.

The Lost Sea is found hidden in a network of caves called Craighead Caverns. The entrance into the cave system is narrow. From this narrow opening the cave expands into a number of very large cave rooms.

The underground lake was a mystery for many years. People had heard rumors that it exisisted, but it was not officially discovered until 1905, when it was discovered by a 13-year-old boy after he went through a hole.

The Lost Sea covers 4 ½ acres and is thought to be the largest underground lake in the world. The lake is available for public viewing. The cave system in which the lake was discovered has been put to use for years. In one room called The Council Room, a large number of Indian artifacts have been found. It is believed by some historians that the artifacts are Cherokee artifacts.

The pioneers are thought to have used the caves for food storage in the 1820's.

Today the cave systems and the Lost Sea are open for public observation. They are located between Knoxville and Chattanooga, Tennessee, off I-75 in Sweetwater, Tennessee. Call 423-337-6616 for more information.

TEXAS
MINI STONEHENGE

How about a visit to a mini Stonehenge? Yes, it may sound strange, but there is a half-sized Stonehenge-- in Texas!

The structure is built on private property; however, people may visit it whenever they wish. The monument brings a bit of the old world to America.

This is an excellent place to stop and have a picnic with your children or to sit and ponder or to stargaze. In some ways, it may be better than going to the actual Stonehenge. How is that? Well, for one thing it may save you from making a trip across the Atlantic and all of the costs related to that. Secondly, the last I heard, the original Stonehenge is fenced off. Thirdly, if children are young enough, they really don't know the difference. It's a good place to give them a short history lesson.

To get there, take Highway 27 to Highway 39. Take Highway 39 to where Hunt Road and FM 1340 connect. The mini-Stonehenge is located at this area.

UTAH
RAINBOW BRIDGE

Hidden in the wilderness, deep on a Navajo reservation, is one of the Creator's best kept secrets. Is it a petrified rainbow? No, it's a spectacular natural bridge.

The natural bridge is called a Rainbow Bridge. It's the largest natural bridge in the world. It is 290 feet tall and 270 feet across. The bridge is remote. There are two trails by which people can hike to the location. They are a 14- mile and a 13- mile trail. The land bridge is near the edge of Lake Powell. It may also be reached by a 50- mile boat trip.

The natural bridge was not even officially discovered until 1909, by the Douglas-Cummings surveyor party. Those who wish to visit the site will never forget it. For more information about Rainbow Bridge, contact Glen Canyon National Resource Recreation Area at 520-608-6404 or the Navajo Nation at 520-871-6636.

VERMONT
ANCIENT WINTER CATHEDRAL

The light of the sun trickles down, making its 93 million mile journey. It spreads through sparkling skies of snow, and makes its way into an age old stone chamber. A door has been opened to greet it on the winter solstice.

Nestled in the wilderness of Vermont, hidden from modern society, is a secret winter Cathedral of the Heavens, or so some say. There sits the stone chamber. Nobody really knows what it is or who built it. Some have said it is an ancient building commemorating the hieroglyphics of the heavens written by the hand of God in the zodiac. They say this because on the winter solstice, the illuminating rays of the sun shine through the entranceway brightening the darkened chamber. Also, they claim the 19 by 10 foot structure contains measurements within that show the lunar cycle. However, no one has really ever proved that this is what the formation was built for. For all we know, it may be a centuries-old potato cellar. Either way, it's an interesting historic relic from another time, another place, another people.

Now you can visit it with permission from the owners. It's on private property. While in Woodstock, Vermont, go south on Route 106 to South Woodstock. Continue through town. When you come to a curve, keep going straight. Go through an intersection for a little over a mile. You'll go up a hill, at the top you'll see a tree with a stone by it. The stone chamber is out in these woods. Get permission to enter.

VIRGINIA
ENDLESS CAVERNS

In Virginia is a labyrinth of caves, a vast network of tunnels known as Endless Caverns. These subterranean passageways are unique in the fact that explorers have never been able to find an end to them.

Ever since the caves were discovered in 1879, scientists and explorers have been trying to chart them. This project has been ongoing to the modern day. At this point, there are over 5 miles of cave passages mapped, and there is no end to them in sight.

There are tours available which will allow you to see Endless Caverns for yourself. This tour takes an hour and 15 minutes. The guide will explain the exploration, geology and history of the cave. To contact Endless Caverns call 540-896-22#. To get to Endless Caverns, take I-81 south to exit 264 (New Market *Ex.)* end of ramp; take a left. Go to second traffic light. Go right on Route 11 for 3 miles, and the cave is on the left.

From I-81 NORTH Exit, 257 go right on Route 11. The caves are 4 ½ miles on the right.

NATIVE AMERICAN ROCK PAINTINGS

Sometime hundreds or perhaps thousands of years ago primitive people painted on rock walls near Yakima, Washington. The paintings can still be seen today.

There are dozens of white and red paintings. Most are human- like faces. The human faces have what appear to be rays of light coming out from around their heads.

There is a pathway that goes along the side of the cliff; from this pathway you can observe the ancient art. Nobody really knows what the faces represent or who actually drew them. There are a number of theories;

However, the possibility exists that these drawings are nothing more than ancient graffiti. In fact, teenagers still paint on rocks in the area.

This historic place is located West of

Yakima, Washington. From Route 82, take Route 12 west for a little over 3 and a half miles. Turn left on Ackley Road. When Ackley comes to an end, turn right on Powerhouse Road. Down the road a ways you'll see the area. For more information call 509-248-0747.

WEST VIRGINIA
DOLLY SODS

How would you like to visit Canada or Alaska? How would you like to do it in West Virginia? If you think this is an impossibility it's not, you can do it at an area in West Virginia called "Dolly Sods."

Dolly Sods is a freak of nature. There are plants that grow there that are usually only found in places such as Northern Canada or Alaska. One such example is reindeer, moss. There are also animals that live there that are usually found in Canada and Alaska -- the snowshoe hair.

Much of the terrain looks like the terrain of the Arctic regions, in the winter. Much of the vegetation has become deformed because of heavy deposits of ice and frost. It's as if a piece of the earth has been misplaced. This section of land seems as if it belongs 1,600 miles further north. However, in the summer temperatures may reach 80 degrees or better. Strange but true.

To get there, follow state route 23 and 55 south to Jordan Run Road. Turn right and go one mile up Jordan Run Road to Forest Road 19. Turn left and follow Forest Road 19, 6 miles to the Dolly Sods Scenic Area.

WISCONSIN
THE LOST PYRAMIDS OF ROCK LAKE

Beneath the surface of Rock Lake, Wisconsin, lie at least 10 ancient structures. These have come to be known as the Pyramids of Rock Lake.

One of the structures is called Limnatis Pyramid. It is estimated that the pyramid has a base width of 60 feet, length of 100 feet, and a height of 18 feet, although only about 10 feet is visible above the murky lake bottom.

Built out of circular black stones, the structure is a truncated pyramid. At the top the stones have a square look to them, and remnants of plaster coating can be seen.

Three miles from the Rock Lake Pyramids is a location called Aztalan. At Aztalan, which was called the Ancient City by early settlers, are two earthen pyramids. Since the early 1800's, archaeologists have believed that the builders of Aztalan may have been related to the inhabitants of Cahokia. Research has revealed that in the past the ancient city covered about 21 acres and is believed to have had a population of approximately 500 people.

Aztalan is located in Jefferson County, Wisconsin.

Off I-94, take exit 259 south. Take Highway 89 into Lake Mills. Go EAST for 2.5 miles on County Highway B, then go south on County Highway Q. The address is N-6264 Highway Q.

WYOMING
THE TOWER

There is a natural landmark in Northwest Wyoming that has been popularized by the movie "Close Encounters of the Third Kind." It is, The Tower.

The Tower is igneous rock and rises vertically from the ground. Its height is 1,267 feet. Geologists say that it was formed by the intrusion of igneous material that eventually eroded away. Beyond that, its formation is a mystery. Scientists are in a state of disagreement over how it came into formation, other than the fact that it was made from igneous material.

Several different Indian tribes consider it a sacred site. Both have their own "theories" concerning it.

While in Wyoming, Route 24 will take you right to the monument.

GEOMETRIC MOUNDS
IN AMERICA

The many mounds of America are interesting in and of themselves. However, there are some researchers who claim that certain earthworks of North America are exhibiting a unique and unusual phenomenon.

Some researchers say that ancient ceremonial mounds of North America are laid out in a geographic order creating geometric patterns.They also claim that Native Americans had the ability to map North America. By placing the mounds at specific coordinates they form interlocking geometric grid patterns, (these create a matrix) that are similar to our current longitude/ latitude system. By connecting the dots (between) ancient mounds, the sites produce patterns that interlace across the United States. For example, some claim that when you take a map and connect various mounds in a straight line, they produce a star pattern. This star pattern goes across the entire eastern United States and covers thousands of miles.

This belief has been at least somewhat confirmed by researchers who have found that some ancient cities have geometric and astronomical alignments that are aligned over a system of several miles. However, most researchers have not conceived of the idea that they may be aligned over a distance of thousands of miles.

There are some who believe that these connections between mounds fit into a much larger picture. This larger picture is explained by what is known as Archaeocryptography, or an ancient code of cryptography. These researchers believe that several thousand years ago, someone mapped out the entire earth. They placed pyramids, mounds, effigy, stone and earthworks at specific locations. Numerology was incorporated into the structure so that when certain measurements were taken of it, it would show the latitude and longitude of where it was placed on the earth. This was all done, according to certain researchers, using the Great Pyramid in Gaza as the prime Meridian.

So the next time you are visiting what some have called an historic American earthwork, you may be looking at a small part of a much bigger structure. Keep in mind that at this point this is only a theory.

EARTH LIGHTS

Did you know there are lighting phenomena that can be observed at various places in the United States? Researchers argue over what causes them.

In certain places strange balls of light appear nearly every clear night and dance around in the sky. They disappear and then reappear. They move and shift, and grow brighter and dimmer. These lights are not to be confused with the Northern Lights. They are, rather, strange and unusual phenomena. Various researchers have different theories about what causes them.

The following is a list of various places you can go to in America to witness this oddity firsthand. These are places where lights appear on a regular basis.

The Marfa Lights, Texas- These lights are some of the best known. They are unique and are located about 9 miles east of Marfa, Texas on Highway 90.

The Brown Mountain Lights, North Carolina- (also known as the Maco Railroad Light). This strange light is seen on a regular basis in Brunswick County in North Carolina. It is 12 miles north of Wilmington on U.S. Highway 74/76. The light is seen near a railroad crossing. The light starts out small and grows to what looks like the size of a swaying lantern.

The Paulding Lights, Michigan- These lights are circular. They are red, white, or green in color. They follow along a set of high wires. They can be seen any night that is not overcast. The lights are located near Paulding, Michigan. To get there, take U.S. 45 north from Watersmeet, or south from Paulding to Robbins Lake Road. Turn west and drive for about a half a mile to the top of a second hill where you will see a barricade blocking the road.

The Hornet Spooklight, Missouri & Oklahoma- This strange light dances, moves around and does various things. It can be seen from both Missouri and Oklahoma. From the town of Hornet, West Hymer Road goes west and ends at State Line Road. From there, the Spooklight area is just to the south on the Missouri side, toward Warren Branch. If you go north on State Line Road, go . 2 mile. Then you can turn west where Oklahoma's East 40 Road begins. Or if you go . 8 mile, you can go west on East 50 Road. According to reports, these are good viewing areas.

The Cemetary lights of Silver Cliff, Colorado- These odd lights at the cemetery dance around various tombstones. Silver Cliff is west of Pueblo on Colorado Highway 96. The cemeteries are about a mile south of town on Mill Street.

The Phantom Lights of Borrego, California- This phenomena occurs from time to time. At this place, balls of fire rise into the atmosphere and then explode like fireworks. This occurs on the northeast end of the Vallecito Mountains, overlooking Borrego Valley on Oriflamme Mountain, above Mason Valley, just north of Vallecito, California.

The Oviedo Lights, Florida- This light show occurs near Oviedo, Florida. A greenish haze of light appears and disappears in late spring and summer. These lights can be seen on Snow Hill Road near Oviedo and Chuluota, Florida.

There are many other lights like this across America. The ones mentioned here are some of the most recurring. This is cheap American entertainment for you and your family.

ILLUSIONS OF GRAVITY

Did you know there are certain places you can go in America where your car will appear to defy the laws of gravity by rolling uphill? Although there are many tourist gimmicks that you can go to, such as shacks built into the sides of hills, that is not what we are covering here. We are not talking about anything man-made. All of the locations mentioned in the following list are naturally occurring. They are free to enjoy.

Gravity Hill Helena, Arkansas - If you happen to be in the area, try coasting up hill with your car at this location. While in Helena, Arkansas, take Highway 49 to Sulpher Springs Road. Get on Sulpher Springs Road at Route 185 and go north. When you top the hill, you'll be looking down at the intersection. You go to the stop sign, and put your car in neutral. From here you will roll uphill about 50 yards.

Gravity Hill California- This gravity defying location is located in Pacoima, California. It is on Paxton Street just off of Fernando Road. Turn off Paxton Street towards a hill. Drive up until you see a split in the road on Paxton, make a left, go up the hill past Foresters Haven. Keep going to the graveyard. Go a little past the graveyard, put your car in neutral, and let your car roll uphill.

Spook Hill Florida Go here and enjoy another illusion of gravity. This place is located between Orlando and Tampa. It is an hour south of I-4 off Highway 27, near Lake Wales.

Booger-Gravity Hill Georgia This freak of nature is located two miles north of Cumming, Georgia. This is about 45 minutes north of Atlanta. It is located north of Highway 9. There is a country road, which goes into a remote area. Once down the road a certain distance, you see two large oak trees. There is a dip in between the trees. Put your car in neutral and your car will look like it's rolling uphill. We suggest contracting a local for more specific directions to this location.

Gravity Hill Indiana This illusion of gravity is located near Mooresville, Indiana, off SR 42 on Keller Hill Road. If you need further help in trying to find this place, we suggest calling the Department of Transportation at 317-831-6509.

Gravity Hill, Michigan- This is a very pronounced illusion of gravity. Your car rolls up an incline hundreds of feet, and stops by an old church at the top of the hill. Take I-75 north to Highway 27 North; take Highway 27 to Highway 10 north, to M-115 north. Follow it to Benzonia, Michigan, to where the highway intersects with Highway 31. Turn left on Highway 31. Go down several miles to Joyfield Road. Go several miles down Joyfield to Putney Road. Turn left on Putney. Drive down to the bottom of the hill, put your car in neutral, and let it coast uphill.

Gravity Hill Pennsylvania Near New Paris,

Pennsylvania. Take Route 30 to Schellsburg. From Schellsburg go north on Route 96 at first traffic light, drive about 4 miles on Route 96 towards New Paris. Just before you get to New Paris, look for a small metal bridge. Just before it, turn left on Bethel Hollow. Drive .6 miles and go left at the Y in the road. After a mile and a half, you'll come to an intersection. Go right on this road and drive two tenths of a mile. Look for GH on the road.

There is a second Gravity Hill three-tenths of a mile past the first. On the right is a telephone pole with the number 69 on it. Call Pennsylvania Visitors Bureau for a brochure at 800-765-3331.

Gravity Hill, Utah- This gravity hill is located a few blocks north by northeast of the Utah state capital. Drive north on Capital Drive, and you will drive down into a canyon. While driving down the main road, another road leaves the main road and goes uphill to the left. However, stay on the main road and drive another 100 feet past that road, and down into the canyon. Put your car in neutral, and roll up hill.

KNOW OF SOME COOL PLACES?

If you have any information about unusual, interesting, or phenomenal places in your state or any other and would like to contribute it to a future addition of **TRIPPING AMERICA THE FANTASTIC**. Please send your information and how we may reach you to:

ZOSMA PUBLICATIONS
P.O. Box 284
Marion, MI 49665